THE
CARROT
COOKBOOK

Varieties text written by
Dr. Peter Crisp of Innovar Plant Breeding

THE
CARROT
COOKBOOK

EDITED BY
NICOLA HILL

Mitchell Beazley

First published in Great Britain in 1995
by Mitchell Beazley
an imprint of Reed Consumer Books Limited
Michelin House, 81 Fulham Road, London SW3 6RB
and Auckland, Melbourne, Singapore and Toronto

ISBN 1 85732 659 8

A CIP catalogue record for this book is available from
the British Library

Printed in Singapore

Acknowledgements

Art Director: Jacqui Small
Executive Art Editor: Penny Stock
Designer: Louise Leffler
Commissioning Editor: Nicola Hill
Editorial Assistant: Kathy Steer
Production Controller: Melanie Frantz
Photographer: Jeremy Hopley
Home Economist: Annie Nichols
Stylist: Blake Minton
Illustrator: Marc Adams

Notes

Both metric and imperial measurements have been
given in all recipes. Use one set of measurements only
and not a mixture of both.

Standard level spoon measurements are used in all
recipes.
1 tablespoon = one 15 ml spoon
1 teaspoon = one 5 ml spoon

Eggs should be size 3 unless otherwise stated.

Milk should be full fat unless otherwise stated.

Ovens should be preheated to the specified temperature
– if using a fan-assisted oven, follow the manufacturer's
instructions for adjusting the time and the temperature.

Storing carrots

If necessary, cut off the leafy tops, then cover loosely
and store in a cool, dark, dry place or in the refrigerator
for 1-3 weeks. Do not keep carrots in a plastic bag or
container. Carrots may turn bitter if stored near apples.

Although they are a traditional crop, carrots owe much of their increasing popularity to the modern food industry. They are easy to grow, with high yields – but the real advantage is that they are brightly coloured. Over the last few decades they have been used extensively in pre-prepared foodstuffs as bulk and as a source of colour. Because there were ready markets for carrots in the food industry, commercial growers and breeders greatly improved the crop, with corresponding benefits to the fresh market crop. Now, good-quality carrots are available throughout the year, and cooks need no longer regard carrots as just another 'boiled root vegetable'.

Originating in Afghanistan as purple and yellow rooted crops, carrots were introduced to north-west Europe about 600 years ago, and the orange type – originally named the Horn carrot – was developed in Holland in the mid 1700s. When the Horn carrot first appeared it was considered attractive enough to figure consistently in paintings by the Dutch Masters. Most modern carrot varieties throughout the world developed from this type. Indeed, the name Horn persists for what are now regarded as quite dissimilar kinds of carrot,

as over the last two centuries the orange carrot diversified according to soils, climates, and tastes. Regional types developed which differed in root size and shape, in the time of season when the root swelled, and in their ability to be stored through the winter.

From the modern breeder's point of view, these different regional types represent a rich source of variability which can be used to construct new types of carrots. The modern 'supermarket quality' carrots have been bred to attract consumers, with bright orange skin and internal colour. The usual tapering shape has largely been bred out of them – most commercial carrots are now cylindrical and 'stump rooted' (that is, with a rounded base). They have also been bred to suit commercial growers, with high yield and uniformity, and enough strength to withstand being harvested by machine. The breeders have managed these advances by recombining the characteristics of regional types from Europe, Japan, Australia and north Africa. Although carrots grown in Europe and the USA are still usually categorized as Amsterdam, Nantes, Paris Market and so on, in reality these usually reflect their shape rather than their origin.

Flavour

The flavour of carrots is partly due to their sugar content. Some varieties of 'baby' carrots have been bred to have an increased sugar content when young. Usually, however, carrot sugars are higher in mature roots, especially if they have been growing in near zero temperatures for a few days.

The main 'carroty' flavour is due to several compounds, such as petroselenic acid, typical of the plant family *Umbelliferae* to which carrots belong (as do parsnip, celery, and several highly flavoured herbs – parsley, coriander, etc). The amounts of these compounds vary according to growing conditions, the age of the root, and to some extent, the variety. Generally, very young roots (baby carrots) make up in texture what they lack in flavour, and are suitable to be eaten raw. Full-grown carrots are available at their best in late summer and autumn, and can be eaten raw or cooked. Carrots which have been stored into or through the winter may need grating to be eaten raw, and they may taste slightly peppery if they have been grown in wet soils: they are therefore probably best when cooked.

Colour

The colour of carrots has no effect on their flavour. However, the orange colour is due to a nutritious class of compounds, usually termed carotenes, which form Vitamin A – vital in humans for normal growth, eye function and resistance to disease, and which may have anti-cancer properties.

The original orange carrots probably had fairly low levels of carotene, but breeders have improved carotene content –

Juwarot

partly by breeding varieties with orange rather than yellow cores. Indeed, during World War II the value of carrots as a source of carotene was recognized, and British breeders doubled the content of carotene in carrots in an attempt to improve the night vision of fighter pilots.

Modern varieties have even higher carotene levels, and current research makes it likely that varieties in a few years' time will have as much as five times more! The variety Juwarot – currently available in both Britain and the USA – is considered to have the highest carotene content.

Pesticides

Commercially grown carrots are usually treated with pesticides to prevent attack by insects, mainly the carrot fly. Because the carrot fly is active through much of the year, these pesticides need to remain active for weeks or months after they have been applied. Carrot growers know when these chemicals will have diminished to levels which are safe for consumers – there is a very large safety margin. However, if you are worried about pesticide residues in your carrots, whether bought or grown in the garden, then peel them just before using them – virtually all of the pesticide remains in the outer tissues.

CARROT TYPES AND VARIETIES

The fortunes of carrots as a commercial crop have burgeoned, and breeding companies are producing dozens of new varieties each year. Nearly all of these varieties are highly uniform F_1 hybrids. Most will be used by commercial growers for five years at most. After that, surplus seed tends to find its way into catalogues aimed at gardeners. Some of these varieties will be very good as amateur crops; however, their availability depends mainly on the 'fall out' from commerce, and for that reason they are not discussed here. Instead, we concentrate on the characteristics of the main types of carrots, and most of the varieties we describe are not F_1 hybrids.

QUICK MATURING

Amsterdam Forcing
This type matures 4-5 months after sowing to give small, tender 'baby' carrots in early summer to early winter.

Amsterdam Forcing

The roots of these carrots are usually slender, cylindrical and stump-rooted, and are often sold tied in bunches with their foliage (which can be used as flavouring in soups). Unlike later-maturing types the young roots tend to develop a good deep orange colour as soon as they start to swell.

The varieties of this type are usually identifiable by the prefixes 'Am-', 'Baby' or 'Mini', or the name 'Finger'; other varieties include Sweetheart and Pampas.

Paris Market
Similar to the Amsterdam Forcing type in most respects, Paris Market carrots are readily recognizable because the roots are virtually spherical, 3-5 cm (*1¼-2 inches*) in diameter.

The type may have derived from the 'French Early Short Horn', which was described a century ago as being 'exclusively adapted for growing in vegetable mould'. The traditional methods of growing high-quality, forced crops around Paris relied on copious amounts

Parmex

of animal and human manure being used to form hot beds.

Carrots grown in highly manured soils are prone to produce forked roots – especially if they are long-rooted types – and it seems likely that increasingly short types were developed to fit in with the Parisian growing methods. Because of its shape, exceptionally among carrots, Paris Market can be transplanted. Varieties often have the prefix 'Par-' (e.g. Parabell, Pariska, Parmex), or have some reference to being round (e.g. Planet, Rondo, Golden Ball, Sweet Cherry Ball, Orbit). Other varieties include Kundulus, Thumbelina and Carpa.

Confusingly, the names Early French Frame and Early French Forcing can refer to the Amsterdam Forcing or Paris Market types.

MIDSEASON

These are the typical fresh market carrots, available from midsummer until early winter.

Nantes
The type is cylindrical, stump rooted, of medium size and usually classed as an early main-

Panther

crop carrot. Much modern breeding has been based on the Nantes type, partly because in its traditional form it lacked the yellow core which typified most other kinds. Its widespread usage is responsible for the common perception nowadays that tapered carrots are something of a novelty.

The Nantes type, because of its attractive features, is usually sold as a prepacked carrot. Modern (mostly F_1 hybrid) varieties of the Nantes type very

often have the prefix 'Na-' or 'Nan-' (e.g. Nairobi, Nantucket). Other varieties include the traditionally named Champion Scarlet Horn and Early Coreless; and a plethora of other named varieties, the best known of which are probably Touchon, Panther, Tiptop and Sytan. The last variety has been found to be less susceptible to carrot fly than others.

The Nantes type has been used extensively to breed improvements into other kinds of

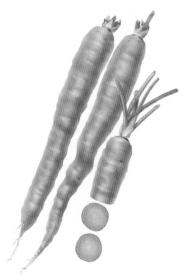

Centennial

carrots, and there are so-called 'Baby Nantes' types, and sub-tropical varieties such as Nantes Mexican. The Nantes has also been used to develop sweet-tasting forcing varieties which are harvested like Amsterdam Forcing, e.g. Sucram, Suko, Sweet 'n' Short, Sweetheart; most are grown commercially for the restaurant trade rather than the fresh market.

Imperator
This type was developed in the USA, is long and slightly tapered, and is mainly grown for the fresh markets.

Most varieties still carry the type name. Other varieties include El Presidente, Falcon, Centennial and Tendersweet.

Chantenay
The Chantenay (still sometimes called 'Early Horn') is conical in shape, although still with a rounded base, and its deep orange colour adds to its appeal. It is medium sized, of medium to late maturity, and is of a good cooking quality, being consistently crunchy rather than fibrous, and is often grown for the fresh market; indeed it has set the standard for commercial-ly grown supermarket varieties.

The type tends to have resis-tance to Alternaria disease.

Some varieties are prefixed 'Red Cored -', and several have 'Red' in their names (e.g. Redca, Long Red), but this is not exclusive to the Chantenay type.

Danvers
This is similar to the Chantenay in most respects, except that the roots are tapered rather than stump rooted. The very old vari-ety James Scarlet Intermediate (also known as English Horn) may be a Danvers type.

Red Cored Chantenay

Danvers

LATE MATURING

Autumn King
This is the 'traditional' type of carrot, being tapered and conical, sometimes with a stump root. It can grow to a very large size, is late in maturing, and is usually grown for the fresh market, often after storage in the field into winter.

Autumn King is a favourite with gardeners because it has a vigorous leaf, which helps

Vita Longa

Apart from those varieties named as Autumn King, the type includes Vita Longa, Campestra, Joba, Carovit, and the Australian variety Flakkee and its derivatives.

Berlicum

These carrots are cylindrical, stump rooted, large, late maturing, and give a heavy yield. The type was used extensively by the Campbell Foods company to breed varieties suitable for their

Camberley

suppress weeds. It also has some resistance to a virus disease, (Carrot Motley Dwarf Virus, which causes leaves to be stunted and a purplish colour, and reduces root size). This probably represents the main type of the otherwise apparently extinct English field carrots (Long Surrey, Long Horn, etc) which, in contrast to the more delicate and finer-quality French types, were grown as large, robust, coarse vegetables as fodder for domestic animals as well as for human consumption.

canned soups, and several varieties have the prefix 'Ca-' (e.g. Camberley, Cardinal). Other varieties include Oranza.

OBSCURE TYPES

Purple-Skinned Carrots

Purple skinned (and sometimes, purple-fleshed) carrot varieties occasionally appear in American and European seed catalogues, usually with names such as 'Afghan Black'. The varieties currently available appear to have little to commend them as they tend to produce flowers rather than roots when grown in northerly latitudes, and few favourable comments have been made regarding their flavour.

Yellow and White Carrots

White and yellow carrot varieties are a traditional cattle fodder in northern Europe. Such varieties are usually available in seed catalogues as 'Blanche (White) Belgian', 'Blanche à Collet Vert', 'White Vosges', 'White French', and 'Lobbericher'. Some are very prone to greening on the exposed roots, and although this is considered a bad trait in orange carrots, greening of carrot roots is harmless (unlike potatoes!). There is evidence

Blanche (White) Belgian

that some of these white and yellow types may have resistance to carrot fly. This apart, there is little reason to favour these varieties – they are generally described as bland, coarse, and susceptible to frost damage.

Oddly-Shaped Carrots
Oddly-shaped varieties are also sold. These include Oxheart (or Guerande), which has very short thick roots – like a Paris Market, but much larger; and St Valery, a variety at least 100 years old, with very long tapering roots. The latter is much favoured for horticultural exhibitions and attempts to grow carrots of record-breaking sizes.

St Valery

CARROT FLY RESISTANCE

A new era in carrot breeding may be dawning as varieties are bred with resistance to the major pest of carrots – the carrot fly, whose maggots eat the roots. The first of these varieties, 'Flyaway', appeared in seed catalogues in 1993, and several more should be released in the late 1990s.

Most have been bred from the variety Sytan and a German white fodder carrot, but some derive resistance from wild relatives of the carrot. The main advantage of these is that little or no pesticides will be needed. However, there may be a downside: insects tend to avoid plants which taste nasty; will the fly-resistant carrots taste as good to humans as the old varieties?

Flyaway

CARROT & LENTIL SOUP

Serves 4-6
25 g (*1 oz*) butter
1 onion, chopped
1 garlic clove, crushed (optional)
2 carrots, chopped
2 celery sticks, sliced
150 g (*5 oz*) red lentils, washed and drained
1 litre (*1¼ pints*) vegetable stock
2 teaspoons lemon juice
about 150 ml (*¼ pint*) milk
2 tablespoons chopped fresh parsley
salt and freshly ground black pepper
croûtons, to serve (see page 18)

Melt the butter in a large pan and fry the onion and garlic, if using, for 5 minutes, until soft but not brown. Add the carrots, celery and lentils and stir around in the butter for a few minutes. Pour in the stock, half cover the pan and simmer very gently for 40 minutes, stirring occasionally.

Pour the soup into a liquidizer or food processor and blend until smooth, or rub through a sieve. Pour back into the cleaned pan and season to taste. Add the lemon juice and thin the soup with milk to the consistency you prefer. Stir in the parsley.

Serve the soup piping hot in individual bowls, sprinkling with croûtons at the last moment.

CARROT & NOODLE SOUP

Serves 4-6
1 tablespoon sunflower oil
1 onion, chopped
750 g (*1½ lb*) carrots, finely chopped
1 teaspoon ground coriander
150 ml (*¼ pint*) orange juice
900 ml-1 litre (*1½-1¾ pints*) hot vegetable stock
50 g (*2 oz*) dried egg noodles
3 tablespoons chopped fresh coriander
salt and freshly ground black pepper
cracked peppercorns, to garnish

Heat the oil in a pan and fry the onion until soft. Add the carrots and ground coriander. Fry for 5 minutes, stirring occasionally. Add the orange juice and 900 ml (*1½ pints*) of the stock. Bring to the boil, lower the heat and simmer, partially covered, for 30 minutes.

Bring a pan of water to the boil. Add the noodles, stir and cover. Remove from the heat and leave for 6 minutes. Drain, then set aside.

Purée the soup in a liquidizer or food processor, or rub through a sieve. Return to the cleaned pan and add the noodles. Stir in more stock if necessary. Add the coriander, season and simmer until heated through. Serve garnished with cracked peppercorns.

Illustrated opposite

FRENCH CARROT BROTH

Serves 4-6
20 g (¾ oz) butter
150 g (5 oz) smoked bacon, diced
625 g (1¼ lb) carrots, sliced
750 ml (1¼ pints) water
2 courgettes, thinly sliced
425 g (14 oz) can cannellini beans, drained
1 garlic clove, crushed
pinch of dried thyme
salt and freshly ground black pepper
1 tablespoon chopped fresh parsley,
to garnish

Melt the butter in a large saucepan. Add the bacon and carrots and cook for 4-5 minutes. Add the water and simmer gently, over a low heat, for about 15 minutes.

Add the courgettes, beans, garlic, thyme, and salt and pepper to taste. Cook over a low heat for a further 7-10 minutes, or until the vegetables are tender.

Sprinkle the soup with chopped parsley. Serve hot with crusty bread, as a filling lunch or supper dish.

CURRIED CARROT SOUP

Serves 4-6
25 g (1 oz) butter
½ onion, sliced
1 garlic clove, chopped
375 g (12 oz) carrots, grated
600 ml (1 pint) chicken stock or water
1 cm (½ inch) piece of fresh root ginger, grated
½ teaspoon curry powder
¼ teaspoon grated nutmeg
¼ teaspoon salt
125 ml (4 fl oz) single cream
freshly ground black pepper
1 tablespoon chopped fresh coriander,
to garnish

Melt the butter in a large saucepan over a low heat. Add the onion and the garlic and sauté gently for a few minutes. Add the grated carrots, stir well, cover the pan and sweat for 10 minutes. Add the stock or water and bring to the boil.

Reduce the heat and add the fresh root ginger, curry powder, nutmeg and salt. Simmer for 30 minutes, then add the cream.

Place the soup in a liquidizer or food processor and blend until smooth, or rub through a sieve. Add pepper to taste. Serve the soup hot or chilled, garnished with chopped coriander.

THE
CARROT
COOKBOOK

CHINESE CARROT & PORK SOUP

Serves 4-6
125 g (*4 oz*) boned lean pork, very thinly sliced
1 tablespoon soy sauce
1 tablespoon sesame oil
1 teaspoon cornflour
250 g (*8 oz*) carrots, sliced
1.2 litres (*2 pints*) chicken stock
2 teaspoons salt
chopped fresh coriander leaves, to garnish

Put the pork in a bowl with the soy sauce, sesame oil and cornflour. Stir well, then cover and leave to marinate for 10 minutes.

Meanwhile, place the carrots, chicken stock and the salt in a saucepan, bring to the boil and simmer for 5 minutes. Add the marinated pork and simmer for 8-10 minutes, or until the pork and carrots are tender.

Pour into warmed soup bowls and sprinkle with chopped coriander. Serve hot.

TOMATO & CARROT SOUP

Serves 4
425 g (*14 oz*) can chopped tomatoes
2 large carrots, grated
1 small onion, finely chopped
300 ml (*½ pint*) vegetable stock
1 teaspoon dried oregano
pinch of grated nutmeg
1 bay leaf
1 teaspoon brown sugar
salt
sprigs of parsley, to garnish

Place the chopped tomatoes and their juice in a saucepan. Add the carrots, onion, stock, oregano, nutmeg, bay leaf, sugar and salt to taste. Bring to the boil, stirring continuously.

Reduce the heat, cover the pan and simmer for 3 minutes. Remove and discard the bay leaf and pour the soup into a hot tureen. Serve garnished with parsley.

VEGETABLES A LA GRECQUE

Serves 4

2 tablespoons olive oil
4 carrots, finely chopped
2 Spanish onions, finely chopped
150 ml (¼ pint) dry white wine
1 bouquet garni
250 g (8 oz) button mushrooms
8 tomatoes, skinned and seeded
salt and freshly ground black pepper
4 tablespoons chopped fresh parsley,
to garnish

Heat the oil in a pan and add the carrots and onions. Sauté until golden. Add the wine and the bouquet garni, and season to taste with salt and pepper.

Reduce the heat and add the mushrooms and tomatoes and a little more wine if necessary. (There should not be too much liquid as the mushrooms will add juice during cooking.) Cook, uncovered, for 15-20 minutes. Remove and discard the bouquet garni, and pour the vegetables into a bowl. Leave to cool, then refrigerate. Serve chilled, garnished with the chopped parsley.

CELERIAC & CARROT REMOULADE

Serves 4

1 celeriac root, about 250 g (8 oz)
2 tablespoons lemon juice
250 g (8 oz) carrots, cut into matchsticks
salt
DRESSING:
4 tablespoons mayonnaise
150 ml (¼ pint) Greek yogurt
1 garlic clove, crushed
1 tablespoon chopped fresh parsley
1 tablespoon finely snipped fresh chives
½ teaspoon mustard powder
pinch of cayenne pepper, plus extra for garnish
TO GARNISH:
1 hard-boiled egg, chopped
snipped fresh chives

Peel the celeriac and cut into matchsticks, dropping into a bowl of water acidulated with 1 tablespoon of lemon juice. Cook the celeriac and carrots in salted boiling water with the remaining lemon juice for 5-8 minutes. Drain, pat dry on kitchen paper and leave to cool.

Mix the dressing ingredients and season. Toss the celeriac and carrots in the dressing, and serve garnished with egg, chives and cayenne.

Illustrated opposite

CARROT & COUSCOUS SALAD

Serves 4-6

250 g (*8 oz*) couscous
2 large carrots, grated
½ red onion, finely chopped
150 ml (*¼ pint*) mayonnaise
salt and freshly ground black pepper
red onion rings, to garnish

Place the couscous in a dish and moisten with warm water. Leave to stand for 10 minutes. Place the couscous in a strainer or metal sieve and steam over boiling water for 15 minutes or until soft. Allow to cool.

Place the cooked couscous, carrots and onion in a large bowl and stir well to mix. Add the mayonnaise and season with salt and pepper to taste. Toss gently to coat and mix thoroughly. Cover and chill until required.

Stir the salad before serving. Serve garnished with red onion rings.

CARROT & WATERCRESS SALAD

Serves 4

6 slices of white bread, crusts removed
2 tablespoons sunflower oil
50 g (*2 oz*) butter
250 g (*8 oz*) carrots, grated
2 bunches of watercress
DRESSING:
grated rind and juice of 1 orange
½ teaspoon sugar
1 garlic clove, crushed
4 tablespoons olive oil
salt and freshly ground black pepper
TO GARNISH:
slices of orange
Danish blue cheese, crumbled

Cut the bread into small cubes. Heat the oil and butter together in a pan, add the bread cubes and fry until golden, stirring frequently. Drain on kitchen paper.

Gently mix the carrots and watercress. To make the dressing, place the orange rind and juice in a small bowl. Add the sugar, garlic, olive oil and seasoning to taste. Stir together well until emulsified, then pour over the carrot mixture and toss well. Sprinkle over the croûtons and serve garnished with slices of orange and crumbled Danish blue cheese.

CARROT & WALNUT SALAD

Serves 4
500 g (*1 lb*) carrots, coarsely grated
1 small onion, thinly sliced
25 g (*1 oz*) walnuts, roughly chopped
50 g (*2 oz*) sultanas
2 tablespoons chopped fresh parsley, to garnish
DRESSING:
grated rind and juice of 1 orange
2 tablespoons lemon juice
3 tablespoons olive oil
1 garlic clove
50 g (*2 oz*) walnuts, roughly chopped
salt and freshly ground black pepper

To make the dressing, put the orange rind and juice, lemon juice, olive oil, garlic and walnuts into a liquidizer or food processor and blend until smooth. Add salt and pepper to taste.

Place the carrots in a large bowl with the onion and mix together. Stir the dressing into the carrot mixture, together with the walnuts and the sultanas. Sprinkle with the chopped parsley before serving.

FRUITY COLESLAW

Serves 6
150 ml (*¼ pint*) natural yogurt
250 g (*8 oz*) white cabbage, finely shredded
2 large carrots, grated
2 green apples, quartered, cored and sliced
2 tablespoons lemon juice
125 g (*4 oz*) seedless green grapes
50 g (*2 oz*) pecan nuts, coarsely chopped
2 tablespoons snipped fresh chives
salt and freshly ground black pepper

Place the yogurt in a large mixing bowl. Season to taste with salt and pepper. Stir in the cabbage and carrots.

Lightly toss the apple slices in the lemon juice and add to the cabbage mixture with the grapes, pecan nuts and chives. Toss well so that all the ingredients are coated with the yogurt and serve.

MARINATED HERBED CARROTS

Serves 4
250 g (*8 oz*) carrots, cut into 4 cm (*1½ inch*)
long matchsticks
1 tablespoon sugar
about 1 tablespoon lemon juice (optional)
salt and freshly ground black pepper
DRESSING:
1 tablespoon tarragon vinegar
¼ teaspoon Dijon mustard
4 tablespoons olive oil
1 small garlic clove, crushed
1 tablespoon finely chopped fresh parsley
2 teaspoons finely snipped fresh chives
1 teaspoon chopped fresh thyme

Place the carrots in a large saucepan. Add the
sugar, ½ teaspoon of salt and just enough
water to cover. Bring to the boil and cook
steadily, uncovered, for 5 minutes. The carrot
strips should retain their crispness.

Meanwhile, make the dressing. Mix the
vinegar and mustard in a small bowl. Beat in
the olive oil, 1 tablespoon at a time, to make a
creamy mixture. Stir in the garlic and herbs.

Drain the carrots and while they are still hot,
mix them with the dressing. Season to taste,
adding more sugar if necessary. If wished,
sharpen the flavour with a little lemon juice.
Chill for several hours before serving.

INDIAN-STYLE CARROTS

Serves 6
50 g (*2 oz*) butter
750 g (*1½ lb*) carrots, sliced
1 potato, peeled and diced
2 teaspoons ground cumin
½ teaspoon chilli powder
1 teaspoon ground coriander
½ teaspoon turmeric
6 tablespoons water
1 teaspoon salt
small sprigs of fresh coriander or parsley,
to garnish

Melt the butter in a saucepan, add the carrots
and potato and fry gently for 5 minutes. Add
the spices, measured water and the salt. Stir
well, cover and simmer for a further 7 minutes,
or until the water has been absorbed.

Serve immediately, garnished with sprigs of
fresh coriander or parsley.

Illustrated opposite

POTATO & CARROT BOULANGERE

Serves 4

500 g (*1 lb*) potatoes, thinly sliced
250 g (*8 oz*) carrots, thinly sliced
1 small onion, thinly sliced into rings
50 g (*2 oz*) streaky bacon, finely chopped
75 g (*3 oz*) Gruyère cheese, grated
300 ml (*½ pint*) chicken stock
a little corn oil
salt and freshly ground black pepper

In a large casserole dish arrange the potatoes, carrots, onion, bacon and Gruyère, in alternate layers, seasoning the vegetable layers with salt and pepper, and finishing with a layer of potato.

Pour in the chicken stock. Cover the casserole and bake in a preheated oven, 200°C (*400°F*), Gas Mark 6, for 30 minutes. Uncover, brush the top with corn oil and bake for a further 30 minutes, or until the potatoes are cooked and browned on top. Serve hot.

VICHY CARROTS

Serves 4

500 g (*1 lb*) young carrots, thickly sliced
150 ml (*¼ pint*) water
15 g (*½ oz*) butter
2 teaspoons sugar
salt
chopped fresh parsley, to garnish

Place the carrot slices in a large heavy saucepan with the measured water, butter and sugar. Cover the pan and cook for 5 minutes, or until the carrots are just tender.

Remove the lid, add a pinch of salt and continue cooking until all the liquid has evaporated, leaving the carrots coated with a syrupy glaze.

Serve the carrots hot, sprinkled generously with chopped parsley.

CARROTS HOLLANDAISE

Serves 4
500 g (*1 lb*) long, thin carrots
a little water or chicken stock (optional)
50 g (*2 oz*) butter
2 teaspoons sugar
2 egg yolks
3 tablespoons double cream
2 tablespoons finely chopped fresh parsley
salt and freshly ground black pepper

Steam the carrots or simmer them in a little salted boiling water or stock until they are barely tender. Put them in a colander and pour cold water over them until they are cool enough to handle. Trim the carrots and rub off the skins. Cut them into 5 cm (*2 inch*) long pieces and then slice them thinly lengthways.

Melt the butter in a pan. Mix in the carrots, sprinkling them with sugar. Cook over a very low heat, shaking the pan occasionally, until the carrots are tender. Beat the egg yolks with the cream. Mix in the parsley and seasoning.

Remove the carrots from the heat. Pour in the egg mixture and stir until thickened, to make a rich, creamy sauce. If necessary, return the pan to a low heat for about 1 minute to allow the sauce to thicken without curdling. Alternatively, stand the pan in a larger one of barely simmering water to finish the sauce. Serve immediately.

ORANGE-GLAZED CARROTS

Serves 4
6 carrots, sliced
3 tablespoons orange juice
1½ tablespoons soft brown sugar
50 g (*2 oz*) butter or margarine
6 whole cloves
salt and freshly ground black pepper
strips of orange rind, to garnish

Cook the carrot slices in a small quantity of salted boiling water until they are just tender but still crisp. Drain and place in a serving dish, keep warm.

Put the orange juice, sugar, butter and cloves into a large saucepan, season with salt and pepper, and heat to simmering point. Remove the cloves with a slotted spoon and pour the sauce over the carrot strips. Leave for a few minutes before serving, garnished with strips of orange rind.

CHINESE CARROT & MUSHROOM STIR-FRY

Serves 4

2 tablespoons sesame oil
175 g (*6 oz*) carrots, cut into matchsticks
1 green pepper, cored, seeded and thinly sliced
250 g (*8 oz*) mushrooms, sliced
250 g (*8 oz*) can bamboo shoots, drained
2 tablespoons light soy sauce
2 tablespoons hoisin sauce
2 tablespoons vegetable stock

Heat the oil in a wok or large heavy frying pan. Add the carrots and green pepper and stir-fry for 1 minute.

Add the mushrooms and cook for 2 minutes, stirring occasionally. Add the bamboo shoots, then gradually stir in the soy sauce, hoisin sauce and vegetable stock. Bring to the boil, simmer for 1 minute, then serve immediately.

CARROTS WITH GINGER & ALMONDS

Serves 4

50-75 g (*2-3 oz*) flaked almonds
2 tablespoons sunflower oil
1 onion, sliced
5 cm (*2 inch*) piece of fresh root ginger, peeled and cut into matchsticks
375 g (*12 oz*) young carrots, cut into matchsticks
4 tablespoons vegetable stock or water
2 tablespoons sweet sherry
salt and freshly ground black pepper

Heat a wok or large frying pan until hot. Add the almonds and dry-fry over a gentle heat, stirring frequently, until golden brown on all sides. Remove from the pan and set aside.

Add the oil to the pan and place over a moderate heat. When the oil is hot, add the onion and ginger and stir-fry for 2-3 minutes or until softened, taking care not to let them brown. Add the carrots, stock or water, sherry and salt and pepper to taste. Increase the heat to high and stir-fry for 3-4 minutes or until the carrots are just tender and the liquid has evaporated. Adjust the seasoning to taste and serve, sprinkled with the almonds.

Illustrated opposite

SWEET & SOUR CARROTS

Serves 4
4 tablespoons sunflower oil
1 cm (½ inch) piece of fresh root ginger, peeled
and finely chopped
500 g (1 lb) carrots, sliced
350 ml (12 fl oz) water
2 tablespoons cider vinegar
1 tablespoon cornflour
1 tablespoon light soft brown sugar
salt
fresh coriander leaves, to garnish

Heat the oil in a frying pan and fry the ginger for 1 minute, stirring constantly so that it does not brown. Add the carrots and stir-fry until all the pieces are coated with oil.

Add 150 ml (¼ pint) of the water to the pan and bring to the boil. Add salt to taste, cover and cook for 5-10 minutes or until the carrots are just tender.

Meanwhile, blend the vinegar, cornflour and sugar together until smooth and mix with the remaining water.

When the carrots are tender, remove the pan from the heat and stir in the vinegar mixture. Return to the heat and stir until the sauce thickens and the carrots look glossy. Serve immediately, garnished with coriander leaves.

BAKED LEMON CARROTS

Serves 4
25 g (1 oz) butter
1 tablespoon soft brown sugar
1 tablespoon lemon juice
500 g (1 lb) carrots, cut into even-sized pieces
300 ml (½ pint) water
salt and freshly ground black pepper
2 teaspoons grated lemon rind, to garnish

Melt the butter in a flameproof casserole dish, add the brown sugar and lemon juice, then add the carrots and stir them into the sugar and juice until they are well coated.

Pour in the water, season with salt and pepper and bring to the boil. Cover the casserole and transfer to a preheated oven, 180°C (350°F), Gas Mark 4. Cook for 20-25 minutes, until the carrots are just tender.

Remove the casserole from the oven, return to the heat and bring to the boil, stirring gently until the liquid has evaporated and the carrots are coated with a buttery glaze. Serve the carrots at once, sprinkled with the lemon rind.

PUREED CARROTS

Serves 4-6

1 kg (*2 lb*) carrots, sliced
pinch of grated nutmeg
40 g (*1½ oz*) butter
150 ml (*¼ pint*) warm milk
1 egg yolk
1 tablespoon tomato purée
salt and freshly ground white pepper
finely snipped fresh chives, to garnish

Bring a large saucepan of lightly salted water to the boil. Add the carrots with the nutmeg. Bring back to the boil, lower the heat and cook gently for 20-25 minutes. Drain the carrots well and place in a liquidizer or food processor with the butter, milk, egg yolk and tomato purée. Season with salt and pepper. Work to a smooth purée.

Return the carrot purée to the clean pan and place over a low heat until heated through and thickened slightly. Spoon the purée into a warmed serving dish and sprinkle with chives. Serve immediately.

VEGETABLE MEDLEY

Serves 4

500 g (*1 lb*) carrots, cut into matchsticks
375 g (*12 oz*) white turnips, cut into
1 cm (*½ inch*) cubes
250 g (*8 oz*) shallots or baby onions, peeled
25 g (*1 oz*) butter
salt

BACON TOPPING:
1 onion, chopped
2 rashers of rindless streaky bacon, cut into
1 cm (*½ inch*) squares
25 g (*1 oz*) butter
6 tablespoons fresh white breadcrumbs
1 tablespoon chopped fresh parsley

Place the vegetables in the top of a steamer or a colander that fits over a large saucepan. Sprinkle with salt and cover the pan. Steam over fast-boiling water for 12-15 minutes, until the vegetables are just tender.

Meanwhile, make the topping. Fry the onion and bacon in the butter for 4-5 minutes, stirring occasionally. Stir in the breadcrumbs and cook for a further 2-3 minutes or until they are golden brown. Stir in the parsley.

Toss the vegetables in the remaining butter and turn them into a serving dish. Sprinkle with the bacon topping and serve hot.

CARROT & ALMOND LOAF WITH TOMATO SAUCE

Serves 6-8

50 g (*2 oz*) butter
1 onion, thinly sliced
2 garlic cloves, chopped
300 g (*10 oz*) fresh wholemeal breadcrumbs
250 g (*8 oz*) carrots, grated
125 g (*4 oz*) flaked almonds, toasted
2 eggs, beaten
4 tablespoons lemon juice
1 tablespoon chopped fresh parsley
1 teaspoon grated nutmeg
salt and freshly ground black pepper

TOMATO SAUCE:
2 tablespoons olive oil
1 onion, finely chopped
1 garlic clove, chopped
425 g (*14 oz*) can chopped tomatoes
2 tablespoons tomato purée
1 tablespoon chopped fresh basil

Melt the butter in a heavy frying pan over a low heat and gently sauté the sliced onion and chopped garlic for about 5 minutes, or until just translucent but not brown.

Meanwhile, in a large bowl, combine the breadcrumbs, carrots and almonds. Add the onion and garlic and stir well. Add the beaten eggs, lemon juice, parsley and nutmeg, season with salt and pepper and mix well. Add a little water if the mixture seems dry, then spoon the mixture into a greased 500 g (*1 lb*) loaf tin and bake in a preheated oven 200°C (*400°F*), Gas Mark 6, for about 45 minutes or until the loaf is nicely browned and a sharp knife inserted in the centre comes out clean.

Towards the end of the cooking time, prepare the tomato sauce. Heat the oil in a frying pan and sauté the chopped onion and garlic for about 5 minutes, or until just translucent. Add the tomatoes, tomato purée and basil and season with salt and pepper, stir well and simmer gently for about 10 minutes. Serve the carrot and almond loaf in slices with the hot tomato sauce.

Illustrated opposite

CARROTS WITH ALMONDS & HORSERADISH

Serves 4

500 g (*1 lb*) carrots, cut into matchsticks
300 ml (*½ pint*) beef stock
50 g (*2 oz*) butter
25 g (*1 oz*) plain flour
2 egg yolks
125 ml (*4 fl oz*) double cream
25 g (*1 oz*) horseradish, grated
50 g (*2 oz*) blanched almonds, chopped
salt and freshly ground white pepper

Simmer the carrots in the beef stock until just tender. Drain, reserving the stock. Keep the carrots warm.

Melt the butter in a saucepan and stir in the flour. Cook gently for 1-2 minutes, stirring constantly. Add the reserved stock, season with salt and pepper and bring to the boil, stirring all the time.

Mix the egg yolks with the cream and stir into the sauce. Remove from the heat and stir in the horseradish and chopped almonds. Finally, carefully fold in the carrots. Serve hot with roast beef or pork.

CARROT & COURGETTE CUTLETS

Serves 4

375 g (*12 oz*) carrots, grated
375 g (*12 oz*) courgettes, grated
50 g (*2 oz*) mature Cheddar cheese, grated
finely grated rind of ½ lemon
2 tablespoons chopped fresh parsley
1 tablespoon snipped fresh chives
2 tablespoons chopped nuts, toasted
6 tablespoons fresh wholemeal breadcrumbs
1 egg plus 1 egg yolk, beaten
plain flour, for dusting
beaten egg, for binding
175 g (*6 oz*) almonds, chopped, for coating
2 tablespoons melted butter
salt and freshly ground black pepper

Mix together the carrots, courgettes, cheese, lemon rind, parsley, chives, toasted nuts, breadcrumbs, egg and egg yolk, and season with salt and pepper. Work together until smooth. Shape into 8 small cutlets, using floured hands. Dip the cutlets into the beaten egg, then coat evenly with the chopped almonds. Chill for 1 hour.

Brush the cutlets on one side with melted butter; cook under a preheated grill for about 5 minutes, then turn the cutlets over, brush the other side with butter and grill for a further 5 minutes. Serve hot.

VEGETABLE CURRY

Serves 4

3 carrots, thinly sliced on the diagonal
175 g (*6 oz*) cauliflower florets, broken into
sprigs, with stalks sliced on the diagonal
125 g (*4 oz*) green beans, halved
125 g (*4 oz*) piece of mooli, peeled and
thinly sliced
2 tablespoons sunflower oil
1 small onion, finely chopped
2.5 cm (*1 inch*) piece of fresh root ginger,
peeled and finely chopped
1 garlic clove, crushed
1 fresh chilli, seeded and finely chopped
1 teaspoon hot chilli powder, or according
to taste
125 ml (*4 fl oz*) water
3 tablespoons crunchy peanut butter
125 g (*4 oz*) frozen peas
salt
40 g (*1½ oz*) dry-roasted peanuts, chopped,
to garnish

Blanch the carrots, cauliflower, green beans
and mooli separately in lightly salted boiling
water, allowing 2 minutes for each type of
vegetable. Drain, rinse immediately under cold
running water and drain again.

Place a wok or large frying pan over a
moderate heat until hot. Add the oil and when
the oil is hot, add the onion, ginger, garlic and
chopped chilli and stir-fry for 2-3 minutes, or
until the onion is soft, taking care not to let
the ingredients brown.

Add the chilli powder and stir, mixing evenly,
then add the measured water and peanut
butter. Bring to the boil, stirring, then add the
blanched vegetables, the frozen peas and salt
to taste. Stir-fry for 3-4 minutes, or until all
the vegetables are tender.

Serve the curry immediately, sprinkled with
chopped dry-roasted peanuts.

VEGETABLE SAMOSA PIE

Serves 6-8

2 tablespoons sunflower oil
1 onion, chopped
1 teaspoon cumin seeds
1 teaspoon mustard seeds
1 teaspoon chopped fresh root ginger
125 g (*4 oz*) carrots, grated
250 g (*8 oz*) potatoes, grated
125 g (*4 oz*) frozen peas
a handful of fresh coriander leaves, chopped
2 tablespoons lemon juice
2 teaspoons curry powder
1 teaspoon ground coriander
¼ teaspoon chilli powder
50 g (*2 oz*) butter, melted
250 g (*8 oz*) frozen filo pastry, thawed
salt and freshly ground black pepper

Heat the oil in a frying pan, add the onion, cumin and mustard seeds and ginger and fry for 5 minutes, or until softened and lightly browned. Add the carrots and potatoes and fry gently for 6-8 minutes, until the vegetables are tender.

Add the peas, chopped coriander, lemon juice and spices to the pan. Season with salt and pepper and stir well. Cook for 5 minutes, stirring, then set aside.

Grease a 25 cm (*10 inch*) square baking sheet and have ready the filo pastry, keeping the sheets of pastry covered while you work to prevent them drying out. Place 5-6 sheets of filo in the centre of the baking sheet, turning each one at a slight angle to the one beneath to form a rough star shape, and brushing each with the melted butter. (The pastry should overlap the edges of the baking sheet by about 10 cm (*4 inches*). If your filo pastry comes in smaller sheets, you can join pieces together, overlapping them by 2.5 cm (*1 inch*).)

Put the vegetable filling in the centre of the pastry. Cover the filling with 3 more sheets of filo, brushing each with melted butter. Draw the bottom filo edges in to the centre to enclose the filling, then scrunch the pastry on top and brush with the remaining butter.

Bake in a preheated oven, 200°C (*400°F*), Gas Mark 6, for 25 minutes, or until the pastry is golden brown and crisp. Serve the pie hot or cold, accompanied by green vegetables or a salad and a bowl of natural yogurt mixed with chopped fresh mint and cucumber.

Illustrated opposite and on page 3

SPICY ROOT VEGETABLE PLAIT

Serves 6-8

50 g (*2 oz*) butter, plus extra for greasing
1 onion, chopped
1 garlic clove, crushed
1 teaspoon grated fresh root ginger
2 tablespoons chopped fresh thyme
1 potato, diced
2 carrots, diced
2 small parsnips, diced
1 tablespoon curry paste
2 tablespoons tomato purée
2 tablespoons mango chutney
150 ml (*¼ pint*) vegetable stock
plain flour, for dusting
500 g (*1 lb*) puff pastry, thawed if frozen
1 egg yolk
1 tablespoon milk
1 tablespoon sesame seeds

Melt the butter in a large heavy saucepan and fry the onion, garlic, ginger and thyme for about 5 minutes. Add the vegetables and continue to fry for a further 10 minutes.

Stir in the curry paste, tomato purée, mango chutney and vegetable stock. Bring to the boil, cover and simmer gently for 15-20 minutes, until all the vegetables are just tender. Set aside to cool.

Meanwhile, roll out the puff pastry on a lightly floured surface to form a 28 x 38 cm (*11 x 15 inch*) rectangle. Transfer to a large greased baking sheet, cover with a clean tea towel and set aside to rest while the vegetable filling is cooling.

Spoon the vegetable filling down the centre third of the pastry. Using a sharp knife, cut slashes along each side of the filling at a slight angle, forming strips about 2.5 cm (*1 inch*) thick. Fold the strips alternately over the filling to make a plaited effect, dampening them with a little water as you go. Press gently in the middle to seal in the filling.

Beat the egg yolk and milk together, brush over the plait and scatter over the sesame seeds. Bake in a preheated oven, 220°C (*425°F*), Gas Mark 7, for 20 minutes. Reduce the temperature to 190°C (*375°F*), Gas Mark 5, and bake for a further 10 minutes. Serve the vegetable plait hot.

CHICKPEA & CARROT PIE

Serves 4-6

PASTRY:

125 g (*4 oz*) wholemeal flour

125 g (*4 oz*) plain flour, plus extra for dusting

50 g (*2 oz*) butter or margarine

125 ml (*4 fl oz*) water

beaten egg, to glaze

FILLING:

2 tablespoons sunflower oil

1 onion, chopped

1 garlic clove, chopped

1 teaspoon chopped fresh root ginger

1 teaspoon mustard seeds

1 teaspoon cumin seeds

4 carrots, grated

175 g (*6 oz*) potato, grated

1 teaspoon turmeric

½ teaspoon chilli powder

150 ml (*¼ pint*) thick coconut milk

50 ml (*2 fl oz*) water

juice of 1 lime

425 g (*14 oz*) can chickpeas or butter beans,
drained

salt and freshly ground black pepper

To make the filling, heat the oil in a saucepan, add the onion and fry for about 5 minutes, until softened and lightly browned. Stir in the garlic, ginger, mustard and cumin seeds and fry for a few minutes more. Stir in the grated carrots and potato, then reduce the heat, cover and cook for about 5 minutes, or until the vegetables are starting to soften.

Stir in the turmeric and chilli powder, then the coconut milk and water. Cover and cook gently for 5 minutes, then remove from the heat. Stir in the lime juice and chickpeas or butter beans, and season to taste. Leave to cool.

To make the pastry, mix the flours together in a bowl. Season with salt and pepper. Heat the butter or margarine and water in a small saucepan until the butter has melted, then stir into the flour and mix quickly to a soft dough. Wrap closely and leave to rest at room temperature for 15 minutes.

Roll out just over half the pastry on a lightly floured surface and use to line a 20 cm (*8 inch*) flan tin, allowing the pastry to overlap the edges. Fill with the cooked vegetable mixture. Roll out the remaining pastry, dampen the edges of the filled pie and cover with the rolled-out pastry. Press the edges to seal, then trim off the surplus pastry and pinch the edges together. Re-roll the trimmings and cut them into carrot shapes. Stick these on the top of the pie with beaten egg, then use more egg to glaze the pie.

Bake the pie in a preheated oven, 200°C (*400°F*), Gas Mark 6, for 35 minutes, until the pastry is crisp and golden brown. Serve hot accompanied by natural yogurt mixed with chopped fresh mint.

PASTA WITH GINGER & CARROT RIBBONS

Serves 4

300 g (*10 oz*) dried pappardelle or other broad egg noodles
2 carrots, scrubbed
25 g (*1 oz*) butter
2.5 cm (*1 inch*) piece of fresh root ginger, peeled and grated
2 tablespoons olive oil
25 g (*1 oz*) pine nuts, toasted
salt and coarsely ground black pepper

Bring at least 1.8 litres (*3 pints*) of lightly salted water to the boil in a large saucepan. Add a dash of oil and cook the pappardelle for 8-12 minutes, or according to the packet instructions, until just tender.

Meanwhile, using a potato peeler, pare the carrots to form flat ribbons. Melt the butter in a frying pan and sauté the carrot ribbons and ginger for 5 minutes.

Drain the pasta well and return it to the clean pan. Toss with the olive oil and salt to taste. Carefully fold the carrot mixture into the cooked pasta. Sprinkle with the toasted pine nuts and coarsely ground black pepper and serve immediately.

Illustrated on front jacket

SPAGHETTI CARROTESE

Serves 4

375 g (*12 oz*) dried spaghetti
3 tablespoons olive oil
6 carrots, very thinly sliced
250 g (*8 oz*) tomatoes, skinned and chopped
3 tablespoons shredded fresh basil
salt and freshly ground black pepper

Bring at least 1.8 litres (*3 pints*) of lightly salted water to the boil in a large saucepan. Add a dash of oil and cook the spaghetti for 8-12 minutes, or according to the packet instructions, until just tender.

Meanwhile, heat the oil in a large frying pan and fry the carrots over a high heat until just cooked, about 5-10 minutes. Add the chopped tomatoes and basil and season with salt and pepper to taste, mixing well.

Drain the pasta thoroughly and return it to the clean pan. Pour the carrot and tomato mixture over the spaghetti and toss well to combine. Serve immediately.

Illustrated opposite

COURGETTE & CARROT PANCAKES

Serves 4-6

PANCAKES:
125 g (*4 oz*) wholemeal flour
½ teaspoon salt
1 egg
1 egg yolk
250 ml (*8 fl oz*) milk
sunflower oil, for frying
150 ml (*¼ pint*) crème fraîche, to serve
snipped fresh chives, to garnish

FILLING:
2 courgettes, grated
1 carrot, grated
125 g (*4 oz*) cream cheese
2 tablespoons snipped fresh chives
salt and freshly ground black pepper

To make the pancake batter, combine the flour and salt in a bowl and make a well in the centre. Add the egg and the egg yolk to the well and whisk, adding the milk a little at a time and gradually whisking in the flour. Whisk until smooth, then pour the batter into a jug and leave in the refrigerator for 1 hour.

Meanwhile, prepare the filling by combining all the ingredients in a bowl.

Heat a very little oil in a small frying pan. Pour in about 2 tablespoons of the pancake batter, quickly tipping the pan so that the batter completely covers the bottom of the pan. Cook gently until the underside is golden brown. Turn the pancake over and cook the other side for a few seconds. Place about 2 teaspoons of the vegetable filling in the centre of the pancake, roll it up and transfer to a lightly greased ovenproof dish. Continue making and filling the pancakes in the same way until you have 12.

To serve, pour the crème fraîche over the pancakes, cover the dish tightly with foil and place in a preheated oven, 190°C (*375°F*), Gas Mark 5, for 10 minutes, until warmed through. Serve immediately, garnished with the snipped chives.

CARROT & TAHINI PANCAKES

Serves 4-6

PANCAKES:

50 g (*2 oz*) buckwheat flour or plain
wholemeal flour

50 g (*2 oz*) plain white flour

2 eggs, lightly beaten

3 tablespoons sunflower oil

150 ml (*¼ pint*) milk

150 ml (*¼ pint*) water

salt and freshly ground black pepper

FILLING:

1 tablespoon sunflower oil, plus extra
for brushing

5 g (*¼ oz*) butter

50 g (*2 oz*) cashew nuts

500 g (*1 lb*) carrots, coarsely grated

300 g (*10 oz*) bean sprouts

1 tablespoon lemon juice

4 tablespoons light tahini

1 tablespoon chopped fresh parsley

To make the pancake batter, combine the flours, ½ teaspoon of salt and a little pepper in a bowl and make a well in the centre. Add the eggs, 1 tablespoon of the oil and half the milk to the well and mix to a smooth paste. Gradually whisk in the remaining milk and the water until smooth. Pour the batter into a jug and leave in the refrigerator for 1 hour.

Heat 1 teaspoon of the oil in a small frying pan until it is smoking hot. Pour in about 2 tablespoons of the pancake batter, quickly tipping the pan so that the batter completely covers the bottom of the pan. Cook the pancake over a medium-high heat for about 2 minutes, then turn it over to cook the other side for about 1 minute.

Make 12 pancakes in this way, adding a little oil for each one. Keep them warm, layered between sheets of greaseproof paper, until they are all cooked.

To prepare the filling, heat the oil and butter in a frying pan and gently fry the cashew nuts for 2-3 minutes, until browned. Add the grated carrots and cook for 3 minutes, stirring occasionally, then add the bean sprouts and cook for a further 3 minutes. Season with salt and pepper, add the lemon juice, then stir in the tahini and parsley. Spoon the filling on to the warm pancakes and serve immediately.

CHICKEN & CARROT RICE

Serves 4

375g (*12 oz*) Basmati rice
1 teaspoon chilli powder
3 skinless, boneless chicken breasts, cut
into strips
75 g (*3 oz*) butter
2 garlic cloves, finely chopped
1 onion, sliced
50 g (*2 oz*) almonds, halved
50 g (*2 oz*) raisins
1 teaspoon turmeric
500 g (*1 lb*) carrots, grated
450 ml (*¾ pint*) chicken stock
salt
sprigs of fresh coriander, to garnish

Wash the Basmati rice thoroughly under cold running water, then soak in plenty of cold water for about 30 minutes. Drain well.

Mix the chilli powder and ½ teaspoon of salt on a plate and lightly dip the chicken pieces in the mixture. Heat 25 g (*1 oz*) of the butter in a frying pan, add the coated chicken strips and garlic and stir-fry for about 2 minutes.

Heat the remaining butter in a large pan, add the sliced onion, the almonds and raisins and fry until golden and lightly browned. Stir in the turmeric, then the drained rice and fry, stirring, for 1-2 minutes. Season well with salt,

then stir in the grated carrots, the chicken strips and the stock. Bring to the boil, cover the frying pan with a tight-fitting lid, reduce the heat to very low and simmer for about 20 minutes or until the rice is cooked and all the liquid has been absorbed.

Transfer the chicken and carrot rice to a large, warmed serving dish and serve immediately, garnished with coriander sprigs.

Illustrated opposite

SOMERSET CHICKEN WITH CARROTS

Serves 4

2 tablespoons sunflower oil
4 chicken portions, skinned
15 g (*½ oz*) butter
2-3 celery sticks, roughly sliced
1 large onion, roughly chopped
2 tablespoons plain flour
good pinch of mustard powder
450 ml (*¾ pint*) chicken stock
450 ml (*¾ pint*) dry cider or apple juice
500 g (*1 lb*) carrots, thickly sliced
1 large bouquet garni
salt and freshly ground black pepper
chopped fresh thyme, to garnish

Heat the oil in a large flameproof casserole dish or heavy saucepan, add the chicken and sauté over a moderate heat for 7-10 minutes, until golden on all sides. Remove the chicken with a slotted spoon and set aside on a plate.

Melt the butter in the casserole, add the celery and onion and cook over a gentle heat, stirring frequently, for about 5 minutes, until softened but not coloured. Add the flour and mustard powder, stir well to mix with the celery and onion, then cook for 1-2 minutes, stirring constantly. Gradually stir in the stock and cider or apple juice and bring to the boil, stirring all the time. Add the carrots, bouquet garni and salt and pepper to taste, then return the chicken to the casserole with the juices that have collected on the plate.

Bring the liquid to the boil again, then cover the casserole and place in a preheated oven, 180°C (*350°F*), Gas Mark 4, for 40 minutes, or until the chicken is tender when pierced in the thickest part with a skewer or fork. Turn the chicken portions halfway through the cooking time, to ensure they are covered in liquid and cook evenly.

Remove and discard the bouquet garni. Adjust the seasoning to taste. Serve the casserole hot, garnished with chopped thyme, accompanied by plain boiled rice or creamy mashed potato.

CARROT & VEAL STEW

Serves 4
2 tablespoons sunflower oil
750 g (*1½ lb*) stewing veal, chopped
1 onion, chopped
1 teaspoon paprika
375 g (*12 oz*) carrots, cut into long matchsticks
2 tomatoes, skinned and quartered
1 dill cucumber, sliced
300 ml (*½ pint*) meat stock
salt and freshly ground black pepper

TO GARNISH:
1 tablespoon chopped fresh parsley
pinch of cayenne pepper

Heat the oil in a flameproof casserole dish or heavy saucepan, add the veal and onion and fry until lightly browned. Season with salt and pepper, add the paprika and cook for about 5 minutes, stirring frequently.

Add the carrots, tomatoes and dill cucumber to the casserole and cook for a further 4-5 minutes. Add the stock and enough hot water to cover the vegetables. Cover the pan and cook over a low heat for about 1½-1¾ hours, stirring occasionally.

Sprinkle the stew with parsley and cayenne pepper and serve with boiled new potatoes or buttered noodles.

CARROT BURGERS

Serves 4
250 g (*8 oz*) extra-lean minced beef or pork
50 g (*2 oz*) fresh white breadcrumbs
1 egg, beaten
25 g (*1 oz*) plain flour, plus extra
for dusting
pinch of ground mace
250 g (*8 oz*) carrots, finely grated
2 tablespoons sunflower oil (optional)
salt and freshly ground black pepper

Mix the mince with the breadcrumbs, beaten egg and flour and season well with salt, pepper and mace. Add the grated carrots and mix together well.

Divide the mixture into 8 portions with lightly floured hands and form into flat burger shapes. Heat the oil in a large frying pan and fry the burgers over a medium heat, turning once or twice, for 10-15 minutes or until cooked through. Alternatively, cook the burgers under a preheated hot grill. Serve hot in burger buns with sliced tomatoes and crisp, shredded lettuce.

NAVARIN OF LAMB PRINTANIER

Serves 4-6

**1 kg (*2 lb*) boned shoulder of lamb, or lamb
fillet, trimmed of excess fat and cut into
5 cm (*2 inch*) cubes
50 g (*2 oz*) plain flour
2 tablespoons sunflower oil
50 g (*2 oz*) butter
250 g (*8 oz*) baby carrots, scrubbed
250 g (*8 oz*) baby turnips, peeled
250 g (*8 oz*) button onions, peeled and
left whole
1 garlic clove, crushed
450 ml (*¾ pint*) chicken stock
2 teaspoons tomato purée
small sprig of rosemary
125 g (*4 oz*) frozen peas
salt and freshly ground black pepper**

Toss the meat in the flour seasoned with salt
and pepper; shake off and reserve any excess
flour. Heat the oil in a large flameproof
casserole dish or a heavy saucepan and fry the
meat briskly on all sides, then remove from
the pan and reserve.

Add the butter, the baby carrots, baby
turnips, the baby onions and crushed garlic to
the pan and fry gently until they are golden
and lightly browned. Sprinkle in any of the
leftover flour and cook gently, stirring, for
about 1 minute. Gradually stir in the chicken
stock, tomato purée and rosemary, and season
with salt and pepper.

Bring to the boil, stirring constantly until the
sauce has thickened and is smooth, then
return the meat to the pan.

Cover the pan, reduce the heat and simmer,
stirring occasionally, for about 1 hour. Add
the frozen peas and continue cooking for
another 30 minutes, or until the meat is
tender. Serve immediately with jacket baked
potatoes and a green vegetable.

Illustrated opposite

ORIENTAL BEEF & CARROT STEW

Serves 4
2 tablespoons sunflower oil
1 garlic clove, crushed
small piece of fresh root ginger, peeled
and chopped
1 shallot, chopped
750 g (*1½ lb*) stewing beef, cut into
1 cm (*½ inch*) cubes
3 tablespoons soy sauce
1 tablespoon sugar
1 tablespoon rice wine or sherry
½ teaspoon five spice powder
500 g (*1 lb*) carrots, sliced on the diagonal

Heat the oil in a large flameproof casserole dish or heavy saucepan. Add the garlic, ginger and shallot and fry over a moderate heat, stirring until golden brown.

Add the beef and the remaining ingredients, except the carrots. Add just enough cold water to cover. Bring to the boil, then cover the casserole, lower the heat and simmer for about 1½ hours.

Add the sliced carrots to the beef stew and simmer for a further 30 minutes, or until tender. Serve hot with mashed potatoes and a green vegetable.

SPICY LENTIL, LEEK & CARROT STEW

Serves 4
1 large onion, chopped
2 tablespoons olive oil
250 g (*8 oz*) leeks, sliced
250 g (*8 oz*) carrots, diced
2 garlic cloves, crushed
1 tablespoon white mustard seeds
1 tablespoon coriander seeds
1 teaspoon turmeric
small piece of fresh root ginger, peeled
and grated
250 g (*8 oz*) split red lentils
900 ml (*1½ pints*) water
1 tablespoon lemon juice
salt and freshly ground black pepper
chopped fresh coriander, to garnish

Gently fry the onion in the oil for 5 minutes, then add the leeks and carrots, stir well and fry for a further 5 minutes. Add the garlic, mustard and coriander seeds, turmeric, ginger and lentils and stir for 2-3 minutes. Then pour in the measured water.

Bring to the boil, then partially cover the pan, reduce the heat and leave the stew to simmer gently for 25-30 minutes, until the lentils are tender. Add the lemon juice and season to taste. Serve sprinkled with the chopped coriander, accompanied by mango chutney and a salad of tomatoes and onions.

COUSCOUS WITH SPICED CARROT STEW

Serves 4

375 g (*12 oz*) couscous

½ teaspoon salt dissolved in 600 ml (*1 pint*) warm water

2 tablespoons olive oil

2 tablespoons chopped fresh parsley

STEW:

2 tablespoons olive oil

2 onions, chopped

500 g (*1 lb*) carrots, sliced

2 teaspoons ground cinnamon

2 teaspoons ground cumin

2 teaspoons ground coriander

125 g (*4 oz*) raisins

2 x 425 g (*14 oz*) cans chickpeas, drained, or

500g (*1 lb*) frozen broad beans, peas or sweetcorn

900 ml (*1½ pints*) water

4 tablespoons tomato purée

salt and freshly ground black pepper

lemon wedges, to garnish

Place the couscous in a large bowl. Add the measured salted water and set aside.

Meanwhile, prepare the stew: heat the oil in a large saucepan or the saucepan part of a steamer. Add the onions and carrots and fry gently for 10 minutes. Add the spices and cook for 2-3 minutes, stirring. Add the raisins and the chickpeas, beans, peas or sweetcorn, the measured water, tomato purée, and season with salt and pepper. Bring to the boil, then reduce the heat so that the stew just simmers.

By this time the couscous will have absorbed the water. Put the couscous into the top part of a steamer, a metal colander or sieve, breaking it up a little with your fingers as you do so. Place the couscous over the stew, cover and steam for 25-30 minutes. Stir the olive oil and chopped parsley into the couscous and serve immediately, with the hot stew. Garnish with lemon wedges.

BAKED CARROT PUDDING

Serves 4-6
4 eggs
125 g (*4 oz*) caster sugar
175 g (*6 oz*) finely grated carrot
75 g (*3 oz*) dried breadcrumbs
40 g (*1½ oz*) ground almonds
¾ teaspoon ground cinnamon
½ teaspoon grated nutmeg
¼ teaspoon salt
1 teaspoon vanilla essence
3 tablespoons melted butter
150 g (*5 oz*) raisins, dusted with
2 teaspoons flour
carrot ribbons, to decorate

Beat the eggs in a large mixing bowl until pale and doubled in volume, adding the sugar a little at a time. Fold in the grated carrot, breadcrumbs and ground almonds, together with the spices, salt and vanilla essence. Stir in the melted butter and raisins.

Pour the mixture into a well-greased 1 litre (*1¾ pint*) heatproof pudding basin. Place the basin in a roasting tin of hot water and bake in a preheated oven, 180°C (*350°F*), Gas Mark 4, for about 55 minutes or until the pudding is completely cooked in the centre. (A skewer inserted in the middle should come out clean.) Turn out, decorate with carrot ribbons and serve warm with custard sauce.

CARROT & APPLE SOUFFLE

Serves 4
50 g (*2 oz*) butter
50 g (*2 oz*) plain flour, sifted
150 ml (*¼ pint*) single cream
½ teaspoon ground cinnamon
2 tablespoons fresh white breadcrumbs
4 eggs, separated
250 g (*8 oz*) carrots, finely grated
250 g (*8 oz*) dessert apples, peeled, cored and grated
40 g (*1½ oz*) walnuts, chopped

Melt the butter in a saucepan and stir in the flour to make a smooth paste. Add the cream and cinnamon and cook over a low heat until the sauce thickens. Cool slightly, then add the breadcrumbs, egg yolks, carrots and apples.

Whisk the egg whites until stiff but not dry, then carefully fold into the mixture.

Pour into greased individual soufflé dishes. Sprinkle over the chopped walnuts and bake in a preheated oven, 200°C (*400°F*), Gas Mark 6, for 15-20 minutes, until well risen and golden brown. Serve immediately.

Illustrated opposite

GRANNY'S CHRISTMAS PUDDINGS

Serves 8 from a large pudding bowl, or 4 from a small pudding bowl

250 g (*8 oz*) sultanas

250 g (*8 oz*) currants

500 g (*1 lb*) seedless raisins

50 g (*2 oz*) cut mixed peel

125 g (*4 oz*) glacé cherries

125 g (*4 oz*) chopped almonds

125 g (*4 oz*) ground almonds

250 g (*8 oz*) fresh brown or white breadcrumbs

2 carrots, grated

1 cooking apple, peeled, cored and grated

250 g (*8 oz*) shredded suet

½ teaspoon mixed spice

pinch of ground or grated nutmeg

½ teaspoon ground cinnamon

250 g (*8 oz*) demerara sugar

grated rind and juice of 1 large lemon

grated rind and juice of 1 orange

250 g (*8 oz*) golden syrup

4 eggs, beaten

4 tablespoons brandy

150 ml (*¼ pint*) brown ale

butter, for greasing

Place all the ingredients in a large mixing bowl and stir well to mix.

Grease 3 x 1.2 litre (*2 pint*) heatproof pudding basins or 6 x 600 ml (*1 pint*) basins well with butter. Fill each basin just over three-quarters full, then cover with greased greaseproof paper and foil or a pudding cloth. Tie securely with string.

Place each pudding in a saucepan and pour in boiling water to come halfway up the sides. Boil for 6-8 hours, depending on the size. Top up with more boiling water as necessary. Remove the puddings from the pans and leave overnight to cool completely.

Remove the coverings and cover again with fresh greased greaseproof paper and foil or a pudding cloth. Store in a cool, dry place away from direct sunlight. These puddings are very moist and will keep well for up to 2 years.

To serve, reboil for 3-4 hours, depending on the size, then turn out on to a warm dish. To ignite the pudding, warm 3-4 tablespoons of brandy in a ladle, pour over the pudding and set alight with a lighted taper. If decorating with a piece of holly on top, wrap the stem in a small piece of foil. Serve with brandy butter or cream.

MOIST CARROT & WALNUT CAKE

Makes an 18 cm (7 inch) round cake

250 g (*8 oz*) soft light brown sugar
175 ml (*6 fl oz*) sunflower oil
2 eggs
125 g (*4 oz*) plain wholemeal flour
1 teaspoon ground cinnamon
1 teaspoon bicarbonate of soda
150 g (*5 oz*) coarsely grated carrot
50 g (*2 oz*) walnuts, chopped

TOPPING:
2 tablespoons apricot jam, sieved
1 tablespoon lemon juice
50 g (*2 oz*) walnuts, chopped

Line an 18 cm (*7 inch*) round cake tin with nonstick baking paper or greased greaseproof paper. (Use a fixed-base tin as the mixture is almost a pouring consistency.)

Put the sugar into a mixing bowl and, using an electric whisk, gradually whisk in the oil, then whisk in the eggs one at a time.

Mix together the flour, cinnamon and bicarbonate of soda and stir into the oil and egg mixture, then add the grated carrot and chopped walnuts. Beat all the ingredients together with a wooden spoon until well combined, then pour the mixture into the prepared cake tin.

Place the cake in the centre of a preheated oven, 180°C (*350°F*), Gas Mark 4, and bake for about 1 hour 10 minutes, or until the cake is risen and firm to the touch. Remove from the oven, leave to stand in the tin for 2-3 minutes, then turn out on to a wire rack, peel off the paper and leave to cool.

To make the topping, boil the apricot jam and lemon juice together in a small pan for 2-3 minutes. Brush the mixture generously over the top of the cooled cake and sprinkle the walnuts over immediately, as the glaze will set very quickly.

CARROT HALVA

Serves 4
500 g (*1 lb*) carrots, grated
750 ml (*1¼ pints*) milk
8 cardamom pods
5 tablespoons vegetable oil or ghee
5 tablespoons caster sugar
1-2 tablespoons sultanas
1 tablespoon shelled, unsalted pistachio nuts,
lightly crushed
300 ml (*½ pint*) clotted or double cream,
to serve (optional)

Put the grated carrots, milk and cardamom pods in a heavy-bottomed saucepan and bring to the boil. Reduce the heat to medium and cook, stirring occasionally, for about 1 hour, or until the milk has reduced by half.

Heat the oil or ghee in a nonstick frying pan. When it is hot, add the carrot mixture. Stir and fry for about 10-15 minutes, until the carrots no longer have a wet, milky look. They should turn a rich, reddish colour.

Add the sugar, sultanas and pistachios. Stir and fry for another 2 minutes. Serve warm or at room temperature with the cream, if using.

SWISS HAZELNUT & CARROT CAKE

Makes an 18 cm (7 inch) square cake
3 large eggs, separated
150 g (*5 oz*) sugar
150 g (*5 oz*) grated carrots
150 g (*5 oz*) hazelnuts, very finely chopped
2 teaspoons finely grated lemon rind
50 g (*2 oz*) plain flour
½ teaspoon baking powder

Well grease an 18 cm (*7 inch*) square cake tin.

Whisk the egg yolks with the sugar until thick and creamy. Stir in the carrots, hazelnuts and lemon rind. Sieve in the flour and baking powder and fold it in. Whisk the egg whites until they form stiff peaks, then carefully fold into the mixture.

Turn the mixture into the prepared cake tin and bake in a preheated oven, 180°C (*350°F*), Gas Mark 4, for 40-45 minutes, until the cake is just firm to the touch. Leave to stand in the tin for 2-3 minutes, then turn out on to a wire rack to cool.

Illustrated opposite

THE
CARROT
COOKBOOK

CHRISTMAS CARROT CAKE

Makes a 20 cm (8 inch) round cake
175 g (*6 oz*) sultanas
4 tablespoons whisky
250 ml (*8 fl oz*) corn oil
125 g (*4 oz*) unrefined molasses sugar
3 eggs (*size 1*)
1 tablespoon cocoa powder
250 g (*8 oz*) plain 85% wholemeal flour
1 teaspoon ground cinnamon
½ teaspoon grated nutmeg
½ teaspoon ground allspice
½ teaspoon salt
1½ teaspoons baking powder
1½ teaspoons bicarbonate of soda
250 g (*8 oz*) carrots, finely grated
75 g (*3 oz*) walnuts, finely chopped

ICING:
375 g (*12 oz*) low-fat soft cheese
50 g (*2 oz*) icing sugar, sifted
finely grated rind of ½ lemon

Place the sultanas in a bowl, pour over the whisky and leave to soak for at least 1 hour.

Line a loose-bottomed 20 cm (*8 inch*) round cake tin with nonstick baking paper, or greased and floured greaseproof paper.

Beat together the oil and sugar, beating in the eggs one at a time. (At this stage the mixture

looks very odd, but don't worry.) Still beating, add the cocoa powder, flour, spices, salt, baking powder and bicarbonate of soda.

Mix in the grated carrots, the whisky-soaked sultanas and any remaining whisky and the walnuts. Stir together well and tip the mixture into the prepared cake tin.

Bake in a preheated oven, 180°C (*350°F*), Gas Mark 4, for about 1¼ hours; a warmed skewer inserted into the centre of the cake will come out clean when the cake is cooked. Allow the cake to cool in the tin.

Place the soft cheese in a bowl and gradually work the icing sugar into it. Add the lemon rind. When the cake is quite cold, spread the icing over the top.

CARROT FRUIT CAKE

Makes a 23 cm (9 inch) round cake
125 g (*4 oz*) soft brown sugar
6 tablespoons clear honey
175 g (*6 oz*) carrots, finely grated
125 g (*4 oz*) seedless raisins
50 g (*2 oz*) stoned dates, chopped
½ teaspoon ground mace
125 g (*4 oz*) butter or margarine
150 ml (*¼ pint*) water
1 egg, beaten
125 g (*4 oz*) plain white flour, sifted
125 g (*4 oz*) plain wholemeal flour
2 teaspoons baking powder

TOPPING:
200 g (*7 oz*) natural quark or low-fat soft cheese
2 tablespoons clear honey
1 teaspoon lemon juice
1 tablespoon chopped walnuts

Mix together the sugar, honey, carrots, raisins, dates, mace, butter or margarine and water in a saucepan. Bring to the boil. Reduce the heat and simmer gently for 5 minutes. Turn into a mixing bowl and leave until cold.

Beat in the egg. Mix together the flours and baking powder and fold into the fruit mixture until thoroughly combined.

Lightly oil a 23 cm (*9 inch*) round cake tin. Line with nonstick baking paper. Turn the mixture into the prepared tin and level the surface. Bake in a preheated oven, 180°C (*350°F*), Gas Mark 4, for 55-60 minutes, or until firm to the touch. Cool on a wire rack.

Beat together the quark or soft cheese, honey and lemon juice. Spread evenly over the surface of the cooled cake and sprinkle over the walnuts.

CARROT & BANANA BREAD

Makes a 500 g (1 lb) loaf
250 g (*8 oz*) plain flour
½ teaspoon salt
1 teaspoon baking powder
125 g (*4 oz*) butter
125 g (*4 oz*) soft brown sugar
1 ripe banana, mashed
2 carrots, grated
2 eggs, beaten

Sieve the flour, salt and baking powder together into a large bowl. Rub in the butter with the fingertips until the mixture resembles fine breadcrumbs. Add the brown sugar.

Combine the mashed banana with the grated carrots and beaten egg and add to the flour mixture. Mix together well, but do not overmix as this will make the texture heavy.

Pour the mixture into a well-greased 500 g (*1 lb*) loaf tin and bake in a preheated oven, 200°C (*400°F*), Gas Mark 6, for 1 hour or until a warmed skewer inserted in the centre comes out clean. Allow the cake to cool in the tin. Serve sliced, with or without butter.

CARROT HEART BISCUITS

Makes 8 large biscuits
150 g (*5 oz*) plain flour, plus extra for dusting
75 g (*3 oz*) butter or block margarine, at room temperature
1 egg yolk
75 g (*3 oz*) carrots, finely grated
caster sugar or icing sugar, for sprinkling

Sieve the flour into a bowl, and rub in the butter or margarine with the fingertips until the mixture resembles fine breadcrumbs. Add the egg yolk and carrots and work together with the hands to make a smooth dough.

Roll out the dough quite thinly on a lightly floured surface and cut out the biscuits using a heart-shaped cutter. Lightly knead any trimmings together and re-roll.

Place the biscuits on a lightly greased baking sheet and bake in a preheated oven, 190°C (*375°F*), Gas Mark 5, for 25-30 minutes, until golden brown. Sprinkle the caster or icing sugar over the biscuits while they are still hot.

Illustrated opposite

COCONUT & PECAN CARROT CAKE

Serves 10-12

200 g (*7 oz*) plain flour, plus 2 tablespoons
for coating
½ teaspoon salt
1 teaspoon bicarbonate of soda
1½ teaspoons baking powder
½ teaspoon ground cinnamon
¼ teaspoon grated nutmeg
3 eggs
250 g (*8 oz*) caster sugar
175 ml (*6 fl oz*) sunflower oil
325 g (*11 oz*) finely grated carrots
2 teaspoons grated orange rind
25 g (*1 oz*) unsweetened desiccated coconut
50 g (*2 oz*) pecan nuts, chopped
125 g (*4 oz*) raisins or sultanas
10-12 pecan nut halves, to decorate

ICING:

1 egg
150 ml (*¼ pint*) single cream
125 g (*4 oz*) icing sugar, sifted
50 g (*2 oz*) butter
125 g (*4 oz*) unsweetened desiccated coconut
50 g (*2 oz*) pecan nuts, chopped

Sift together the flour with the salt, bicarbonate of soda, baking powder and spices and set aside.

Beat the eggs with an electric mixer, gradually adding the sugar, and beating until the mixture is thick and pale. Slowly pour in the oil, beating constantly until it is completely absorbed, then fold in the flour mixture, a third at a time.

Toss the carrots, orange rind, desiccated coconut, pecan nuts and raisins or sultanas with the remaining flour, then stir into the cake mixture. Pour into a greased 18 x 28 cm (*7 x 11 inch*) or 20 x 30 cm (*8 x 12 inch*) tin. Bake in a preheated oven, 180°C (*350°F*), Gas Mark 4, for about 45 minutes, until a warmed skewer inserted in the centre comes out clean. Leave to cool in the tin.

Meanwhile, make the icing. Beat the egg and cream together with the sugar. Place in a saucepan with the butter and cook over a moderate heat, stirring constantly, for about 7-8 minutes, until thickened. Remove from the heat and stir in the desiccated coconut and pecan nuts. Set aside to cool.

Spread the cooled icing over the cake. Cut into squares, place a pecan nut half on each square and serve.

CARROT JUICE

Makes 4 small glasses
500 g (*1 lb*) carrots, finely grated
50 g (*2 oz*) sugar
4 tablespoons lemon juice
600 ml (*1 pint*) cold water

Place the carrots in a bowl and sprinkle with the sugar and lemon juice; leave to stand in a cool place for a few minutes.

Add the measured water, stir well and leave to stand for 1 hour.

Pass the carrot juice through a sieve and chill until required. Serve the juice as it is or use as a basis for Carrot Flip (see right).

CARROT FLIP

Makes 4 small glasses
250 ml (*8 fl oz*) Carrot Juice (see left)
300 ml (*½ pint*) single cream
4 egg yolks
125 ml (*4 fl oz*) fresh orange juice
crushed ice
thin slices of orange, to decorate

Put the carrot juice, cream, egg yolks and orange juice into a cocktail shaker and mix well. Alternatively, place the ingredients in a bowl and whisk to combine thoroughly.

Pour into tall glasses containing crushed ice and serve immediately, decorated with slices of orange.

Illustrated on page 1

CARROT RAITA

Makes about 200 ml (7 fl oz)
2 young carrots, grated
1 tablespoon grated onion
150 ml (¼ pint) natural yogurt
2 tablespoons olive oil
1 teaspoon orange juice
1 teaspoon ground coriander
½ teaspoon cumin seeds, crushed
2 teaspoons finely chopped fresh dill
pinch of ground cardamom
salt and freshly ground black pepper

Put the grated carrots in a large bowl, add the grated onion and stir together. Add all the remaining ingredients, season to taste and mix thoroughly until well blended.

Cover the bowl with clingfilm and chill in the refrigerator for about 30 minutes.

Serve the chilled raita with grilled meat or oily fish such as mackerel.

CARROT & ORANGE CHUTNEY

Makes about 1-1.5 kg (2-3 lb)
375 g (12 oz) carrots, grated
250 g (8 oz) onions, thinly sliced
250 g (8 oz) cooking apples, peeled, cored and grated
175 g (6 oz) soft brown sugar
50 g (2 oz) raisins
2 whole cloves
grated rind and juice of 4 oranges
450 ml (¾ pint) cider vinegar

Place the carrots, onions and apples together in a large saucepan with the sugar, raisins, cloves and grated rind and juice of the oranges. Pour over the vinegar.

Bring to the boil, then reduce the heat, cover and simmer for 40 minutes. Remove the lid and simmer for a further 40 minutes, until the chutney is fairly thick.

Meanwhile, sterilize and have ready warmed jars. Pot the chutney, leave for a few minutes, then cover tightly and label.

Serve the chutney with cold meats, poultry or bread and cheese.

Illustrated opposite

SPICY MIXED VEGETABLE RELISH

Makes about 1.5 kg (3 lb)
250 g (*8 oz*) aubergines, halved lengthways
175 g (*6 oz*) onion, grated
250 g (*8 oz*) carrot, grated
250 g (*8 oz*) tiny cauliflower florets
1½ tablespoons salt
450 ml (*¾ pint*) cider vinegar
150 ml (*¼ pint*) water
175 g (*6 oz*) soft dark brown sugar
1 teaspoon coriander seeds
½ teaspoon ground ginger
1½ teaspoons curry powder
15 g (*½ oz*) pickling spice, tied in muslin
125 g (*4 oz*) frozen sweetcorn
125 g (*4 oz*) frozen peas
25 g (*1 oz*) flaked almonds
1 tablespoon cornflour
2 tablespoons water

Cut the aubergines across into very thin slices. Put into a large bowl with the grated onion and carrot, the cauliflower florets. Sprinkle the salt over the vegetables. Pour in enough water just to cover the vegetables and leave to stand overnight.

Next day, drain the vegetables well and squeeze with the hands to extract as much water as possible.

Put the vinegar, measured water, sugar and all the spices in a pan, bring to the boil, then lower the heat and simmer for 20 minutes.

Add the drained vegetables, sweetcorn, peas and almonds to the pan, cover and simmer for 10 minutes. Remove the lid and boil fast for about 7 minutes, then remove the muslin bag of pickling spice.

Blend the cornflour and water together until smooth and stir into the pan. Boil the relish for a further 3 minutes, stirring until thickened. Pour into warmed sterilized jars, seal and label. Serve with grilled or cold meat or poultry.

CARROT & SEVILLE ORANGE MARMALADE

Makes about 2.75 kg (5½ lb)
625 g (1¼ lb) Seville oranges, thoroughly
washed and halved
1.2 litres (2 *pints*) water
1 kg (2 *lb*) carrots
1 kg (2 *lb*) sugar

Squeeze the juice from the oranges and reserve. Collect all the pips and tie in a piece of muslin. Cut up the peel fairly coarsely and place it, with the juice and the bag of pips, in a large bowl. Pour over the measured water, cover the basin and leave overnight.

Next day, place the orange mixture in a large pan, bring to the boil, then reduce the heat and simmer gently until the peel is quite tender and the weight of pulp is 1.25 kg (2½ lb). Remove and discard the bag of pips.

Cook the carrots in 600 ml (*1 pint*) of water in a covered saucepan until tender. Drain the carrots, reserving the cooking water, then purée the carrots in a liquidizer or food processor, or rub through a sieve.

Add the carrot purée and the reserved cooking water to the orange mixture, bring to the boil, add the sugar and boil rapidly for about 1 hour, until it is a fairly thick consistency.

As this marmalade contains little sugar it will not keep longer than a week or so unless hermetically sealed. This may be done by pouring the marmalade into hot sterilized jars and sealing with waxed discs, placed wax side down. The covered jars should then be immersed while hot in a pan of hot water, brought to the boil, and boiled for 5 minutes. The marmalade will then keep for months.

Illustrated on page 2

— THE —
CARROT
INDEX